'It's desire not ability that determines our success'

Richard Denny

Dedication

To my dad, he wasn't with us long enough but taught me from an early age the importance of knowing your numbers.

To the Zulu nation, who were treated so appallingly by the British Empire, and all the lives lost on both sides in the Anglo Zulu War of 1879.

Contents

ABOUT THE AUTHOR

Joe Hinton, founder and Managing Director of UK Business Mentoring Ltd started his working life in 1973 as an apprentice dental technician. That lasted for all of three weeks until he was told that this particular occupation had the highest suicide rate of any profession. This coupled with the fact that he struggled to walk in 'Dr Scholl' sandals, the chosen footwear of dental technicians in the 1970's, was motivation enough to try something different. There followed a thirty-five-year career in banking.

He formed UKBM in 2009 which provides mentoring support to small businesses across the UK. This also includes undertaking complete reviews of businesses using his copyrighted 'Zulu Business Model'.

Regular seminars run by the company give insightful practical advice and information to small business owners to help them in both the day to day running of their business and also growing it, with possibly, a view to selling at some stage.

Joe is a practiced public speaker and enjoys bringing levity and storytelling to his presentations which reflects his long-held desire to be a standup comedian!

This is unlikely to happen now, as it's hard to fit it all into one lifetime.

Foreword

This book is based on my experiences over the first ten years of coaching, mentoring, supporting, guiding, being the shoulder to cry on, and the guy to call for numerous small business owners. Their names will not be mentioned, and the stories have been changed to protect the innocent, where necessary.

I hope that the content of this book will help the group of people that I truly admire, small business owners who are fundamentally vital to the economy and the future of our great nation. I also hope it will be useful to and maybe even inspire those, who are at the start-up stage with their business or indeed those who have been trading for years.

I am indebted to the many small business owners who have attended my seminars and especially those who have let me in to their businesses and shared part of their lives with me.

A particular thank you to my wife Deborah who despite me offering an ear to everyone but her at times, smiles, encourages me and makes me want to be a better man every day.

What the Zulus taught us about business

Introduction

Consider this, I had completed 35 years in banking; I had been that old style 'Mr Mainwearing from Dad's Army' Bank Manager. I had experienced being a pillar of the community, someone who people would come to for help and advice and most importantly someone people trusted. Moreover, I had made it to 'Bank Manager' at the ripe old age of thirty-three, in those days that was young. Nowadays it is old, in fact I think one of the qualifications to be a Bank Manager these days is to be experiencing the early signs of puberty.

Anyhow I digress, somehow by 2004 I had managed to blag myself into the reasonably elevated position of Regional Director, my responsibilities stretching along the south coast and up to Suffolk. How I managed to rise to that level still baffles me. I had managed to side step ever taking the 'Institute of Bankers' (a thrilling name if ever there was one) exams and I confess here and now I have never passed an exam in my life. Now this will come as a surprise to my old employers, who if they ever check the records will see that every year on my 'Annual Report' I claimed to have five 'GCSE's' or 'O Levels' as they were in my school days.

So, time to confess, when originally interviewed for the job in 1973, I lied. The very austere gentleman asked me how many O Levels I had obtained and I (knowing the minimum required was four) replied "five" He countered with "What subjects?" and without hesitation I offered up "Maths, English, English Literature, Biology (I felt qualified as had recently lost my virginity) and woodwork. Clearly the last one was a little desperate, but I felt the magazine rack and cigarette box I had lovingly crafted for my parents under the scornful eye of Mr Heywood, my woodwork teacher gave me the right to this claim. I do remember Mr Heywood reviewing my handiwork and commenting "Hinton, I hope you have a brain in that head of yours because you will never make money with your hands"
"Thank you, sir."

Anyhow back to the point, I had grown to enjoy the advantages of being a 'Bank Official' I could sign off passports, even shotgun certificate applications, I was trusted and respected.

Then came the new millennium and an increasing demand for companies, and banks to provide more and more 'shareholder value' in simple terms make as much profit as possible at the same time maintaining customer satisfaction levels. Now in reality, what this meant was ramming poorly designed and sometimes expensive products down customers throats. PPI comes to mind here.

As the poor customer popping in to pay in their £25 premium bond prize cheque would find, "Do you know when your home insurance renewal date is?" "Shall we open a credit card for you to make it easier to spend your winnings?" "We could show you how we can save you money on your mortgage and if we can't we'll give you a box of Maltesers".

I as the Regional Director would then collect the daily sales figures from a group of keen Area Managers and would join a daily conference call to relay the days 'spoils', oops sorry sales figures to my Managing Director.

I did actually pride myself, and so did my team of Area Managers on doing it the right way and encouraging our staff in branches to do the same. In reality of course, there was 'mis selling' going on. I recall a manager who was encouraging his staff to, upon notification of the death of a customer, convert the account to a packaged account (which attracted fees) after all "Who was going to complain"?!

In terms of the customer service, I felt as a whole the bank was playing lip service to it, too many cases of "Mr Customer, if you bring your customer service survey into us to complete with you, we'll give you a box of Maltesers"
What was it with bloody Maltesers?

Staff numbers were being cut, queues were growing, scandals seemed common place and the whole fabric of a once respected institution was slowly crumbling before my eyes.

The realisation that it was time for me to move on came on one conference call when tired of collecting the daily sales 'booty' numbers I decided to test my area managers ability to do 'dolphin' impressions. When this was followed the next day by a request to mimic the sound of a ``llama' (now that's a tricky one), I knew it was time for me to move on.

There followed a few months of negotiating 'favorable terms' for my request to depart the bank and I shall always be indebted to my old boss for supporting me with this. In fact, he encouraged me, pointing out "The bank needs clones now Joe, not personalities". So, at the ripe old age of fifty one, in June 2009 I was leaving as a 'Pensioner' which gave me numerous benefits, aside from a pension, invites to pensioners tea parties, walks through Kew Gardens and discounts on various mobility aids.

I had in mind a different destiny for myself.

For the first weeks of 'retirement' I visited the gym each day which was followed by chatting to very nice ladies in the hot tub, but I soon became aware that, as a daily visitor I was in danger of becoming the 'hot tub nuisance' so that had to end.
That time did give me the opportunity to consider what I would like to do next. The two areas that really gave me satisfaction, and I felt I was pretty good at during my career had been coaching and mentoring staff and working with owners of small businesses. It didn't take me too much thinking time and, I didn't need those five fantasy O levels to realise that coaching and mentoring business owners was the future for me.

I then spent a few weeks undertaking some market research for my new business idea which included running a seminar for thirty business owners. This highlighted this group of people needed and indeed wanted help across a number of areas that I could provide.

And so, a business was born, and UK Business Mentoring started trading on the 24th September 2009.

These books are designed to be a source of reference (and hopefully a damn fine read too!) for the small business owner to help him or her with their personal journey of development. It's a fact that as your business grows, so does your role as business owner change. Initially maybe you were a sole trader, doing everything yourself, but as the business grows you will need to develop your skill set and learn to do a lot more 'managing' than 'doing'.

It is a journey that will be full of frustration and set back but one that will also bring enormous satisfaction and potentially great financial returns.

Over the last ten years one of the statistics that has become apparent is that for the owner started and managed business there is commonly a point at which early success has been replaced with frustration and some disillusionment. That point I have found to be around the £1m/£2m turnover level and in between the 5-25 employees, irrespective of industry.

My conclusions on this are that the motivated, passionate, driven business owner gets his/her business to those levels largely on their hard work and determination and are, to a large extent still involved in a lot of the 'doing'.

The frustration comes as the business owner, having recruited staff finds that things are not done as well as they would expect. Standards slip, they are spending long hours in the business but it's all starting to feel a little out of control.

The typical reasons for this are that staff are not managed effectively, people do not have a clear view of their role and what their objectives are within the business. Nobody is sitting down with them and highlighting all the good things they do or indeed the things that need improving. Sometimes the financials are not well managed and key performance indicators (KPIs) are ignored (more on this later). We also find that the owner has not put in place a structure and is not delegating or empowering his/her people.

Another area typically ignored is marketing, 8/10 businesses we work with have no marketing plan.

So, in summary the common areas we find need addressing in this size of businesses are:

- Leadership & Management of People
- Financials
- Marketing & Sales

If any of this resonates with you and you now realise 'it's not just you', then please get in touch. With a good Mentor on board a lot of the above can be made far less painful.

'Scaling' Your Business

ukbm

There is a direct correlation between the growth of a business and the changing role of the owner

A Brief History Lesson

In January 1879 Britain suffered one of its worst defeats against a native force. If you have seen the famous 1963 film starring Michael Caine, you will know it was the Zulus.

In December 1878, unknown to the British Government, the High Commissioner, Sir Henry Frere gave the King of the Zulus, King Cetshwayo, a deadline to disband his army. Not surprisingly, given they had not instigated any hostilities, other than minor border disputes, towards the British, they did not comply.

In January 1879 Frere sent a column of approx. six thousand red coated British troops led by Lord Chelmsford into Zulu land to destroy the Zulu army.

On the 22nd January, Chelmsford split the column into three, two columns were sent to find the Zulu army (thought to be around 20,000 in strength), and the third comprising of around 1500 men was left at base camp, next to Mount Isandlwana.

The British soldiers at camp were said to be 'spooked' by the similarity of the shape of Mount Isandlwana to their collar badge showing the Egyptian Sphinx, they felt it was a bad omen and indeed it was.

Mount Isandlwana

The 24th Regiments 'Sphinx' collar badge

Later that day the camp was attacked by a force of some twenty thousand Zulus. Despite being heavily outnumbered, the British, in theory, should have been able to hold off this mighty army. The red coats had the latest state of the art single shot breech loading rifles 'Martini Henrys' which given a rate of fire of around ten shots per minute and a range of up to a mile. This combined with the devastating effects of 'volley fire' should have stopped the Zulus who were attacking across over a mile of open terrain. The British camp was however overrun by the Zulus and all, but a handful of lucky escapees survived.

So how did the Zulus, armed with spears and shields and a few old rifles manage to defeat a professional, well trained and disciplined army, equipped with the most modern weapons available at the time?

Aside from incredible bravery, no doubt fueled by anger at their country being invaded for no good reason, a formidable battle tactic known as the 'Impondo Zankomo' the 'Beasts Head' or `Buffalo Horns' played a great part in their victory that day.

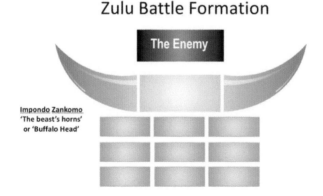

Zulu Battle Formation

The main head of the army made up of experienced married warriors would attack first, engaging the enemy and keeping them fully employed. The horns of the buffalo, consisting of the younger single warriors would then move around and out-flank the enemy on both sides and eventually join up, thus fully encircling their enemy.

Simple, but absolutely deadly.

After Isandlwana one of the 'Buffalo horns' made up of around 4,000 warriors went on to attack the British supply post and hospital a few miles away at Rorkes Drift. This was the battle made famous in the wonderful (although not entirely historically accurate) film starring Michael Caine and Stanley Baker 'Zulu'.

At this battle, around one hundred and thirty British soldiers held off the Zulu attack until after 24 hours the Zulus relented and moved on. Following this encounter, Victoria Cross Medals (the highest honour in British military terms) were awarded to eleven of the defenders, the highest number of VCs ever awarded in a single action.

For the record, let us not forget the bravery of the Zulu warriors, who, after all, were defending their country against an invading force and suffered horrific losses.

There are, I am pleased to say monuments in memory of both the British and Zulu warriors who lost their lives in these encounters at the sites today.

Memorial to the Zulu warriors who lost their lives

Memorial to the British soldiers who lost their lives

The Zulu Business Model

So how does this help my business I hear you ask?

Well, at UK Business Mentoring we believe that the Zulu's 'Horns of the Buffalo' tactic can be used as a model to guide business owners. The model covers what your business should look like to be in shape and prepared for growth (battle!) and how it can be used to 'attack' your market place and indeed your competitors.

Our version of the 'Buffalo Head' is shown overleaf.

ZULU BUSINESS MODEL

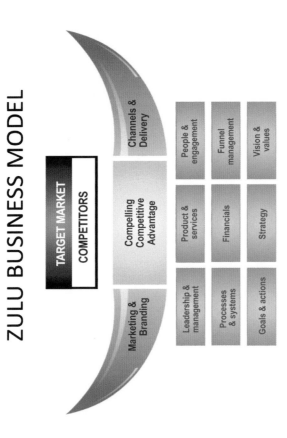

ukbm

22

We use the model as a way of verifying that all component parts of the business are fit for purpose. There is very little point in working on growing one's business if there are flaws in it – for example, you can spend a fortune on marketing to attract new enquiries, but if you're not dealing with the existing enquiries effectively then you are in danger of wasting a whole heap of money.

Over the last ten years we have helped over three thousand business owners by using the model, either via seminars (where 96% of the attendees would strongly recommend the seminar), or via 1:1 working with clients.

One book covering all areas of the Zulu Business Model would be one mighty tomb indeed, therefore we have created a series of smaller, more manageable books to enable the reader to digest bite-size chunks

To make the book (hopefully!) a more engaging read, the information and advice around areas of the Zulu business model are told through a variety of real-life case studies, stories and anecdotes.

The first element of the Zulu model I am going to start with in this book is 'Funnel Management' The reason for this is that it contains lots of information and advice as to how to make quick improvements in the profitability of a business. This has been an area of keen interest to the majority of business owners at our seminars over the years and therefore I feel, will be a key area for you the reader and a suitable subject for the first book.

Throughout the book you will see various boxed elements marked with the symbol shown below (shaped like a Zulu shield of course!) highlighting a top tip. These are areas where we have found that large numbers of our clients who implement these points gain most benefit in terms of an increase in net profit.

We therefore strongly recommend that to get the maximum benefit out of this read you act on these points.

Using Numbers To Find Love

Thirteen years ago, I found myself in the position of being a single man again after many years of marriage. Where was I, a man in his late forties going to find a partner again? All my friends were married with families and were unlikely to want to join me on nights out frequenting clubs and bars looking for *love*. Cheeky Pete's discotheque in Richmond, my haunt from the early 70's was no more, so that was another angle closed off to me.

The answer was of course Online, to join the millions of people looking for that perfect person on the internet.

So, having done my research, I joined Match.com.

There were two ways of making contact with people whose profile you liked, 'winking' at them (they got a message to say you had winked at them) but this did seem somewhat shallow and reminded me somewhat of Sid James leering over women and giving them a cheeky wink in all those Carry-on Films of the 1960/70s.

The other option was to send them a message/email and somehow put across your 'interest' and see if they responded favorably. This was the option I chose, and I quickly found that a well-crafted and somewhat amusing email gained the best response.

Coming from a sales background, I soon noticed that there was a trend developing, for every twelve emails sent I would get back three replies. Two of those would be positive (the other one being a polite no thank you - clearly a look at my profile picture had killed off any chance of a connection there.

From those two replies I would then respond suggesting we chat on the phone and from those two calls, generally one person would be put off by the others voice or 'manner' and the second one we would result in a first date.

Normally, that first meeting 'date' would be just for a coffee or quick drink.

There is a good reason for that, I had, early on in this new world of online dating found that you should never agree to meet for a meal or anything more than a 'quick drink'. On several occasions I found myself committed to dinner, which can obviously last one or two hours, only to be sat opposite someone who I had absolutely no attraction to and indeed they clearly felt the same. But here were we, two strangers being very polite to each other, knowing that if our paths never crossed again for eternity it would be a result.
So, dear reader, I hear you asking but what in the name of all things business-like has this got to do with my business?

The answer is *knowing your numbers*.

I knew that twelve emails gave me three responses (25% conversion) which gave me two telephone calls which then gave me one date. Using the good old sales funnel approach, I could therefore plan ahead. If sending twelve (well crafted) emails gave me one date (conversion rate approx. 8%) then twenty-four would give me two and so on.

I could plan how many first dates I wanted for two weeks' time and so on. All the time knowing that the more first dates I went on the greater my chance of finding 'Miss Right'.
And it worked, on my 75th first date I met Deborah, my wife (and mum to our gorgeous daughter) and we both knew from that 'quick lunchtime drink in the pub' that turned into lunch and then a few more drinks, five hours in total, that we were a 'match'.

So, 900 emails had given me around 225 replies, which in turn resulted in around 150 telephone calls and 75 first dates.

I was a man on a mission and knowing my numbers had made the whole process seem more achievable in my head. Now of course, the one formula I did not know was the conversion from first date to finding love. For me it turned out to be one in 75, for others it would be different, and two clients come to mind here that I introduced to online dating. Both ended up marrying the first date they went on! I wish both of them very many happy years and also that I had been on commission.

I have on occasion referred to my wife Deborah as 'Miss 75' and in fact once bought her a T shirt with number 75 emblazoned in crystals across the back. For some reason she never saw the funny side of it.

The message in the story is about the benefit of knowing your numbers and in my experience many owners are not close enough to their numbers – their 'KPIs' (key performance indicators)

With this in mind I am going to explain our 'Business Dynamics Funnel' which includes the only six KPIs that will grow your profitability. This is one area that will genuinely *pay you* to focus on as *small* improvements here can make *HUGE* improvements in profits!

Business Dynamics

Funnel Management

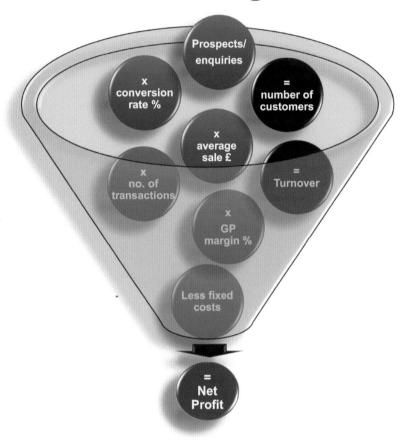

The Business Dynamics Funnel

The six blue balls represent KPIs, each one of them can improve the profitability of your business, the maroon balls are outputs, i.e. a result of the blue balls. If you think of your annual accounts which show the annual turnover or 'sales' for your business, the first four blue balls show how that figure was arrived at so:

Annual turnover or sales =

No of enquiries (Ball 1)

x your conversion rate of % (Ball 2)

= the number of customers you transacted with

x the average sale (your average invoice value or Total sales divided by number of invoices/sales) (Ball 3)

x number of transactions (the number of times your customers purchase from you) (Ball 4)

= Your turnover £

We then use the last two balls to arrive at your net profit:

Multiply the turnover figure by your gross profit margin % (Ball 5) to arrive at your Gross Profit £

Deduct your annual fixed costs (Blue ball 6) and you are left with your net profit £

When we first go through these six areas with clients, we normally work through balls 2-6 first and then come back to ball 1, why would you think that is?

It's because it is generally accepted that it is far harder (some say seven times more difficult) to get a new customer rather than do more with an existing one. Therefore, we work on improving all areas around 'existing enquiries' first and then move on to looking at how to get new enquiries.

As mentioned earlier there is no point in attracting lots of new enquiries until you are certain that the existing ones are being maximised.

The Power Of Conversion

Funnel Management

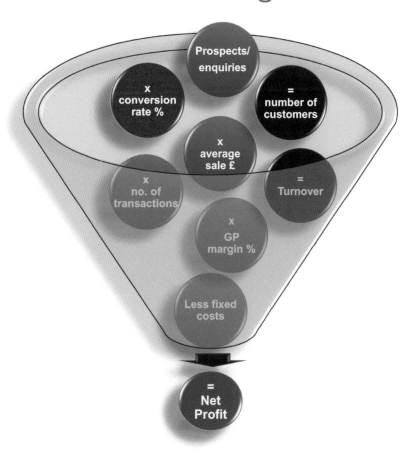

So, we start with number 2, the percentage conversion rate from enquiry to buying customer. Very few businesses keep an accurate enquiry record to track this information and most business owners will guess at their conversion rate based on their 'gut feel'. If you don't keep such a record then start to, it will give you invaluable information going forward. You should also track the 'source' of the enquiry so you can establish which area of your marketing is giving you the best results.

Calculate your Enquiry Conversion Rate:
Number of new customers divided by Number of enquires X 100

Example 1

William was the owner of a franchised domiciliary care company, providing carers for the elderly and those in need of some kind of support at home. Telephone enquiries would come in and after taking some basic information about the person needing care (phone calls were normally from a family member) a time and day would be arranged for an 'assessment' This consisted of one of the two supervisors visiting the home and meeting the individual with their family member(s) and assessing the persons care needs. This would include such things as number of care visits required per day/week and the level of support to be given.

When we started with this owner, he was not tracking enquiries and therefore what happened to them. At our suggestion he tracked them for a month and at our next meeting was pleased to show us the excel spreadsheet showing that from sixteen enquiries last month they had obtained eight new care packages i.e. new clients. William was pleased with the 50% conversion rate.

When digging under the numbers however we pointed out that of the two supervisors, one had signed up seven of her eight enquiries and the other only one from eight. He decided to track for a second month to 'get more data'.

The second months cumulative figures showed the differential even more starkly, the first supervisor had converted sixteen of eighteen enquiries (a conversion rate of 88%) and supervisor two had achieved two out of seventeen (12%), a combined conversion rate of just over 51%.

To reinforce the potential effect on the business we did a quick calculation.

Based on the two months data, in a full year, supervisor two would see approximately one hundred potential customers and at her current conversion rate of 12% would convert twelve into new clients.

If we overlaid Supervisor one's conversion rate of 88%, where 88 sign ups would be achieved that's potentially seventy-six lost clients per annum.

The average new care package in the business was £480 per month or £5,760 per annum. Therefore losing 76 new clients on an annualised basis equates to £437,760 per annum.

At the businesses gross profit margin of 42% that is a loss of gross profit of £183,859 per annum, and assuming no increase in fixed costs that's £183,859 of net profit lost to the business!

So, let's say we could improve Supervisor two's conversion rate to 50%, that's an increase in signups from 12 to 50, an increase of 38.

$$38 \times £5,760 = £218,880 \text{ per annum}$$
$$\times \text{Gross margin of } 42\%$$
$$= £91,929 \text{ Gross profit and again assuming no increase in fixed}$$
costs that's £91,929 of extra net profit per annum!

So maybe now you can see why we focus on what's happening to the existing enquiries first?

William arranged for his Care Manager to undertake some observations with Supervisor two to ascertain why the conversion rate was so low. It transpires that whilst there was some mitigation, in as much as the business did have some capacity issues in her geographic area (shortage of carers so packages couldn't be committed to) The main reason however was how the individual presented both herself and the company at the meeting. It was not professional and did not come across in the empathetic way that families in the difficult position of arranging care for their loved ones would expect.

Some coaching was provided to Supervisor two and her conversion rate improved to over 50% for several months but then began to deteriorate again and following formal performance procedures she resigned from the company. The business continues to thrive, William has recently purchased a second territory from the franchisor and is still a client today.

Example 2

Back in 2010, I was introduced to Vernon and Sandra who had several years earlier purchased an existing large London based children's nursery. Historically the business had been very profitable but over the last year or two profitability had dropped, and the business was having cash flow issues, indeed the Revenue were chasing hard for outstanding PAYE arrears.

The owners blamed the downturn on the effects of the recession and felt that parents just couldn't afford child care fees.

Now, when parents are considering a nursery for their child there are several psychographics (reasons to buy) that come in to play. Speed, quality of response to the enquiry, whether by phone or website are important as is the latest Ofsted (Office for Standards in Education, Children's Services and Skills)
report on the business. However, in my experience, the two key factors are price and above all the quality of the nursery as seen by the parents when they go on a visit to the nursery, a 'show around' After all, if you're leaving your loved one in strange new surroundings, in someone else's care you want to be comfortable with the environment and above all the carers.
Vernon and Sandra didn't track the enquiries and therefore didn't know their conversion rate.

We persuaded them to track their enquiries including where they came from (web/recommendation etc.) what percentage then came on a 'show around' and then the percentage of those who registered their child for a nursery place.
We also arranged to mystery shop the nursery to test how it felt from a prospective mum's point of view.

During the first month of tracking, seventeen enquiries were received, the vast majority of which were via the website contact form. Of those enquiries, six (35%) came on a show around and three (17.6%) registered for a place. So, nearly 1 in 5 people who enquired have on the face of it chosen a different nursery.

Let's once again look at the financial implications of these conversion rates.

The average fees paid by parents at this nursery was then £900pm, £10,800pa. The average takes in parents who have just one or two days care per week and those who have anything up to a full five days.

So, based on one month's figures of seventeen enquiries and three 'registrations', if changes could be implemented which would improve the conversion rate to say 33%, we would sign up five (rounded down from 5.6) rather than three. That would bring in two extra registrations per month which on an annualised basis is an extra twenty-four children per annum, so:

2 X £900 = £1,800pm or £21,600 per annum
Annualised 12 X 2 registrations per month = 24 extra per annum
24 X £10,800 = £259,200 per annum
£259,200 turnover times by gross profit margin of 46% = £119,232 extra NET PROFIT (as no extra fixed costs required)

So, the low conversion rate was costing the business circa £120k of net profit!

Our mystery shopper highlighted the following positives and negatives following the show around:

Positives

- Information pack, once received was comprehensive and included all required information
- The various age-based rooms in the nursery appeared well kitted out
- There is a lovely grassed outdoor area and many outdoor facilities
- The basement is a large soft play area that looks great fun
- The Nursery kitchen has a five-star rating

Negatives

- Information pack took ten days to arrive following web enquiry
- No phone call follow up from Nursery, I had to ring them
- I was only given the choice of one day and time for a 'show around'
- The member of staff seemed very short on the phone
- The Manager who conducted the show around with us seemed very stressed and was continually interrupted by staff asking her questions
- The whole show around felt rushed and we felt somewhat of a 'nuisance'
- Some areas of the nursery looked tired and needing redecorating
- When the show around finished, we were shown to the door and told, 'Give me a call if you want to register' there was no discussion around what days/hours of care we needed for our child

On the back of all this information the following actions were agreed:

- Another member of staff (an existing deputy manager) was trained (by us) to deal with all enquiries and show arounds, which were booked at a day and time to suit the parents

- A pdf of the information pack was put on the website for parents to download once their details had been entered (name, email, phone numbers) thus negating the need to wait for the post.

- Immediately the web enquiry form was received the deputy manager would make contact with the parents on the phone to arrange a convenient time for a show around with an email confirmation. If unavailable on the phone an email would be sent with a further call in 24 hours and then 48 hours.

- The show around by the Deputy Manager was extended to 45 minutes and included a walk around all the rooms and explanations of what activities the children were involved in and how they linked to the curriculum. The visiting parent's child was also encouraged to get involved in the room's activities with the other children.

- At the end of the visit the parents were taken to the soft seated area of the nursery, where letters from delighted parents are displayed, to discuss their care needs for their child.

- Certain areas of the nursery were repainted in bright vibrant colours.

In addition, some of the Nursery Managers duties were delegated to other staff to relieve the pressure on her.

The costs involved in the above changes were minimal, the web company made the downloadable pdf changes as part of their existing maintenance charge and the only additional costs were some tins of paint and the owners time at a weekend to do the painting.

This business has since grown its turnover by £500k (up 70%) and improved its net profit from £34k to £325k through, increasing the enquiry conversion rate to consistently over 35% and other activities such as:

- Introducing an effective Google pay per click campaign (driving enquiries from 200 to over 400)

- Registering on National Nursery websites (for referrals)

- Managing staff numbers/wages to consistently under 48% of income (and well within staff to child ratios)

Vernon and Sandra are still clients to this day and in 2017 opened a second site.

Example 3

Jarvis is the owner of a high-quality clothing company that we have been working with since 2009. Initially they sold on a wholesale basis to retailers but following our suggestion began offering products via a new ecommerce website direct to consumers. This clearly brings a far higher gross profit margin than wholesaling and was essential to growing profitability and the brand.

One of the early challenges with the website was the high cart abandonment rate `(people putting products in their 'basket' and then not completing the sale). Initially, the abandonment rate was almost 80%, so four out of five people who picked a product(s) from the site dropped out when it came to making payment.

Encouraging Jarvis to visit his own website and make a purchase, which it has to be said he was initially reluctant to do as he explained "I can just pop into the warehouse and help myself" helped highlight the issue.

Once the product selection was made and you moved to the 'check out' there were three pages of information to complete. This combined with a confusing breakdown of cost which made it appear that VAT was still to be added to the price when in fact it was included, was clearly putting people off.

Reducing the check-out pages to just one and making the actual price you were going to need to pay crystal clear improved the abandonment rate from 80% to 40% within days.

The financial implications were as follows:

Circa 100 visitors per month at 80% drop out rate = 20 sales
Circa 100 visitors per month at 40% drop out rate = 60 sales

So, an extra 40 sales per month at an average sale value of
£126 = £5,040 per month
X 12 = £60,480 per annum

At a gross margin of 70% =
£42,336 extra NET PROFIT per annum

In summary, I hope that these examples give you an idea of the importance of both tracking and taking action on your conversion rate. Also, they highlight why it is worth investing time into this ahead of undertaking a lot of marketing to attract new enquiries.

So, our top ten tips for analysing your businesses conversion rate are shown overleaf.

1. Analyse in detail your process from initial enquiry right through to sale and indeed the after sales process (which we cover later in the book)

2. Look at all the paperwork involved in the process and also listen, if you can, to the people involved in the process e.g. the person taking the phone enquiry

3. Get someone to mystery shop your business, how was the experience for them? What was good and bad? Would they have purchased? What could be improved?

4. Mystery shop your competition; how well do they do? What could you learn from them?

5. Lay out in process map form what you want/expect your process to be so that it is absolutely clear

6. Arrange for your staff to be coached/trained by you or someone else on why the change is necessary and how to actually undertake the process

7. Track your enquiries and what happens to them

8. Set conversion objectives/targets for the staff involved

9. Meet with the staff at least weekly initially to check on progress

10. **Lastly, never assume the process is happening unless you have seen it for yourself**

The Incredible Effect
of
Chocolate And Fries

Funnel Management

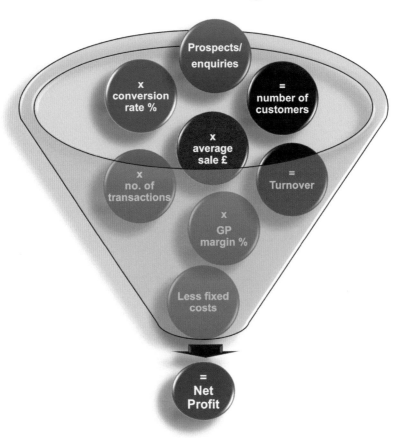

Do you recall when you last popped into a branch of WH Smith and picked up the latest copy of 'Goat Herders Monthly' or whatever publication or newspaper floats your particular boat. What happened when you reached the checkout?

You were probably offered a large bar of chocolate for the very reasonable price of £1.

Now we all know why they want to sell us more but, have you ever considered that by this single sales technique alone they are probably making around an extra £7.5 million PROFIT each year?

When this last happened to me I chatted to the cashier about the offer and she told me that most people just say "No thanks`' but about one in ten will buy the chocolate.

As of February 2018, WH Smith had over 1400 outlets worldwide across 27 countries but for the purpose of this example let's focus on just the UK high street stores of which there are 610.

Now let's assume the average number of sales in a UK store is just five hundred per day (I'm sure it could be far more) then let's apply some mathematics to it:

500 sales per day x 610 stores = 305,000 sales per day in the UK
If one in ten people buy that bar of chocolate that equates to 30,500 bars sold per day for a total of £30,500

Now let's assume the chocolate bars cost WH Smith thirty pence each (probably less)
That's 70p profit per bar or a gross profit margin of 70%
Multiply the daily sales of choccie bars of £30,500 by 70% gives

Extra NET PROFIT of £21,350 per day
OR
Around £7.792 Million NET PROFIT per annum!

Do you see why WH Smiths try to sell everyone a bar of Galaxy? (other chocolate bars are available and offered ☺)

Now consider the world's second largest employer (behind Walmart). With over 36,000 outlets and 235,000 staff across 100 countries McDonalds is phenomenal. You may love or hate them, but I feel you have to respect them as a business if only because they serve 69 million people every day (about 10% of the world's population!).

Visiting a McDonalds and asking for a Big Mac or whatever delicacy has excited your taste buds that day would invariably provoke a response of "Would you like fries with that"
Let's consider the implications of that simple question.

Assume that question, to everyone who just orders some kind of burger on its own, is asked of one in ten customers and that lets say just a half of customers respond with yes please.
The numbers look something like this:

69 million customers
1 in 10 asked the question = 6.9 million
50% say yes = 3.45 million
Multiply by the cost of fries, say £1 = £3.45 Million
Gross profit margin on fries – say 80% (probably more)
£3.45 million x 80% =£2.76 million NET Profit Per DAY
Or just over £1 BILLION per year!

A Billion pounds profit by just getting teenage kids to ask the question "Would you like fries with that?"
And these are the same teenage kids that we can't get to take their plate into the kitchen!

Take the WH Smith example, by selling a bar of chocolate at £1 to one in ten customers how much do they increase their average sale by?

The answer is 10p (£1 divided by 10) and this may seem like a very small amount but multiply it up by the number of transactions shown in the example above and the effect is huge.

These examples are to highlight our second 'Ball of Profitability' 'Average Sale'.

How do you work out your average sale?

> **Calculate your Average Sale:**
> Total sales in £ divided by number of sales
> (both ideally over the previous twelve
> months)

Why is knowing what your average sale is so important?
Because if you know what it is you can decide on actions to improve it and any increase will have a really positive impact on bottom line profit.

Q. What is one very simple way of increasing your average sale?

A. Increase your prices

Now this is quite a controversial subject, many business owners are reluctant to increase their prices because of the fear of losing customers. The largest influence on what dictates the price you charge is probably what the market dictates. Now all markets will have their own factors that will influence price, the cost of supplies/raw goods being one. Our clothing company mentioned above were influenced by the cost of wool and cashmere. In my experience however one of the main factors in determining price in many small businesses is confidence.

Five years ago, I was asked by a family member if I could help a friend of hers who runs a small café in a Sussex market town and who was apparently struggling to make any money.

I spent one Saturday morning down there, initially strolling round looking at her competitors of which there were three. I had a discussion with the lady for about an hour whilst watching her serve the customers, many of whom were obviously regulars from the very friendly nature of the conversations she was having with them.

This was a very small café, just two tables to sit at inside, a couple outside but the majority of the business was takeaway. All the prices for food/drinks were attractively presented on a blackboard measuring around 8' by 3' high up behind the counter.

The thing I immediately noticed was the prices, for example a large latte coffee was £1.50. When I had 'mystery shopped' the competitors earlier I had noticed the large latte prices were between £2.10 and £2.40. Other products had similar price differentials.

I enquired why her lattes were priced at that level and she told me she didn't think her clients would stand an increase and also, whilst pointing to the blackboard said "We had the blackboard prices painted on professionally five years ago, it would cost a lot to get it repainted!"

I sat down and did a few sums with her based on the fact that she knew on average she was selling seventy-five lattes per day (her electronic till provided the information)

Assume a price increase to the lowest competitor of £2.10
An extra 60 pence per cup
60p X 75 lattes per day = £45 per day extra income
Multiply by 7 days open per week = £315 per week extra NET PROFIT as no increase in costs at all
Which equates to £1,312 per month or £15,750 per annum (based on 50 weeks) extra NET PROFIT

On just ONE product!

The lovely lady was quite shocked by the numbers, but I could still detect a reluctance driven by a fear of losing customers. We discussed why her regulars were regulars and she agreed it was about her friendly welcoming way with each of them so why would they move to a competitor who was going to charge the same (if she increased) or more?

She agreed to test out new prices on just two products for a month, £2.05 for a latte and £5.95 for a full English breakfast (previously £4.95 – nearest competitor £6.95).

After one month we spoke on the phone, how do you think her regulars had responded to the price changes?
She told me she could not see that she had lost one customer and the only comments had been along the lines of "I never understood why you were so cheap!"

Very much around confidence and of course….the cost of a tin of blackboard paint!

So, let's look at how businesses in general should arrive at the price for their products and in these examples, we are not including any businesses that have a truly original product and can virtually dictate their price. Nor are we covering the big brand names such as Apple whose brand (and quality of products) can dictate a price far in excess of their competitors. Consider the cost of an iPad vs. other much cheaper rivals.

Firstly, and importantly, consider what the product costs you to have it ready to sell. So that will include cost of the goods or raw material, cost of labour or other costs to finish the goods ready for sale. Then you need to decide on what your 'mark-up' will be i.e. how much are you going to add to the cost of the product before you sell it. This will undoubtedly also be driven by what your competitors will charge. Although don't assume it does, if you're the very best in your market then people will generally pay more.

It's worth mentioning at this point that 'mark-up' is a very different measure to 'gross profit margin', many people get confused by the two.

For example, imagine the cost to you of one of your products is 50p and you 'mark it up' by 100% to £1. The actual gross profit margin for this product will be 50% calculated as follows:

Sale £1
Less cost of goods 50 pence
= Gross profit of 50 pence

Calculate the gross profit *margin* as follows:
Gross profit divided by sales x 100
So…
50p divided by 100 pence = 0.5
X 100 = 50%

The following table highlights the difference between 'Mark-up' and 'Gross profit margin'

'Mark-up' Vs Gross Profit margin %

Mark-up	Vs	GP Margin
15.00%	=	13.00%
20.00%	=	16.70%
25.00%	=	20.00%
30.00%	=	23.00%
33.30%	=	25.00%
40.00%	=	28.60%
43.00%	=	30.00%
50.00%	=	33.00%
75.00%	=	42.90%
100.00%	=	50.00%

Check your Mark-Up/GP margin %
Using the above chart plot your product mark-up against your gross profit margin

Whilst looking at price increases it's also worth mentioning the effects of *reducing* prices. On many occasions this is done for good reason e.g. a sale, Black Friday, Xmas Sale, Summer sale to clear out last season's stock or a special offer to attract more customers. All good reasons as long as the business owner understands the implications of reducing prices. When you reduce prices, you in effect reduce your gross profit margin for the period of the 'sale' which means you need to sell more to make the same profit and sometimes a whole lot more to make any more gross profit.

Here is a table that highlights the effects of reducing prices:

Funnel Management

The effect of *reducing* prices

	Existing % Gross Margin								
	5	10	15	20	25	30	35	40	50
% Price Reduction	% Volume increase required for same gross profit								
2	67	25	15	11	9	7	6	5	4
3	150	43	25	18	14	11	9	8	6
4	400	67	36	25	19	15	13	11	9
5		100	50	33	25	20	17	14	11
7.5		300	100	60	43	33	27	23	18
10			200	100	67	50	40	33	25
15				300	150	100	75	60	43

ukbm

The chart shows, based on your current gross profit margin and what % you reduce your prices by, what percentage increase in sales you require just to make the same 'Gross Profit'

So, if your business has a gross profit margin of 40% and you intend to reduce your prices by 10%. The graph shows you will have to sell 33% more just to make the same level of gross profit.

Worth considering before you reduce your prices?

Conversely, here is a similar chart but showing the effects of *increasing* your prices:

Funnel Management

The effect of *increasing* prices

% Price Increase	Existing % Gross Margin								
	5	10	15	20	25	30	35	40	50
	% Volume decrease to generate same gross profit								
2	29	17	12	9	7	6	5	5	4
3	37	23	17	13	11	9	8	7	6
4	44	29	21	17	14	12	10	9	7
5	50	33	25	20	17	14	12	11	9
7.5	60	43	33	27	23	20	18	16	13
10	67	50	40	33	29	25	22	20	17
15	75	60	50	43	37	33	30	27	23

The chart shows, based on your current gross profit margin and what % you increase your prices by, what percentage *decrease* in sales you could tolerate to make the same 'Gross Profit' i.e. this shows the 'buffer' you have in terms of losing customers due to a price increase.

So again, if your business has a gross profit margin of 40% and you increase your prices by 10% the graph shows you could afford to lose 20% of your sales to make the same level of gross profit.

The real benefit of increasing your prices is of course that typically this involves no extra costs so the increased revenue this generates goes straight on to your bottom-line net profit.

Worth considering reviewing your prices?

I should explain that I am not suggesting you wish to lose customers but rather highlighting the 'risk' in terms of lost sales volume. Sometimes however, there are customers that maybe you would like to or maybe should lose. Those service hungry customers who maybe take up more time than you think necessary, did you ever review the true cost of dealing with these 'heart sink' customers? (so, called because that is the feeling you get when you see their name or number appear as an incoming call!)

There is also an understandable reluctance amongst small business owners to increase prices and risk losing customers. I always recommend looking at your prices in conjunction with what your competitors charge and the quality of what you deliver versus those direct competitors. At the end of the day the question for you (and also your customers) is 'Is what you're providing worth paying more for?'

So, having calculated your own average sale on page 52 how can you increase your average sale?

Let's consider that mighty online sales retailer 'Amazon'. Each time you look at a product on their site/application you will get a box showing you that the particular item is 'Frequently bought together' with an associated item(s). So, for example while writing this I am viewing a Yale Home Alarm system priced at £187.93. It automatically offers me an extra PIR and key chain remote for the system I am looking at. This has the effect of potentially increasing my purchase to £229.53. At the same time, it shows me a newer model, priced at £299.99 for me to consider. It also shows me separately at the bottom of the page "Customers who bought this also bought' various other accessories.

This is the ultimate average sale increasing 'machine'.

Now looking at your business, how can you increase your average sale?

Ask yourself the following questions:

What other products or services that you offer or *could offer* would your customers find useful?

> **Consider other Products or Services**
> What else might your customers be interested in purchasing from you?

Could you introduce your customer to another provider who could offer a complimentary product that you could receive commission on?

Can you offer a supermarket style buy three and get one free or buy one and get 25% off the second?

Whilst writing this I am reminded of when I was first 'single' again and had moved into a new property. In the first week I returned home one evening and managed to snap the front door key off in the lock' I couldn't get the broken piece out, so I called a local locksmith. He arrived within thirty minutes and quickly retrieved the broken end from the lock. I asked him if he could change the lock, as the old one seemed to be hard to open. He obliged explaining that the new lock would be £90 with three new keys.

Within minutes he had completed the work and handed me three new keys and invited me to test the lock.

Now that morning, I had been running one of our seminars for business owners. One of my favourite sections of it is around 'Average Sale' so my head was still filled with this 'stuff'.

So, with all this in mind I thought let's try and help this owner of a locksmith business.

As he tidied up to leave and I paid his bill, I asked him "So, what else do you think you could do for me?"

Now to be honest my question was followed by a few awkward moments as he looked at me quizzically and it occurred to me that he could be thinking I was 'coming on to him'.

I therefore quickly added "to make my property secure". He looked suitably relieved. I followed with "Could you check out my conservatory and other ground floor windows and door locks to see if you think they are adequate, I am out most days and would like to know my home is secure".

He then examined the various side and rear doors and conservatory and made suggestions as to how mortice locks and additions to the conservatory doors would be more secure. He gave me. A price of £140 and proceeded to do the work – all done in forty minutes. In that time, he had (or rather I had) increased his average sale from £90 to £230.

By the time he had finished I had drafted out by hand on an A4 piece of paper, a 'home security checklist' including such lines as 'check strength of all door locks' 'open and close all downstairs windows to check locks' 'consider outdoor security lights'.

I showed him this and suggested that when visiting client's home's, he offers a free home security review, he could use the checklist with clients to highlight any security shortcomings.

This would of course increase his average sale but would also be a great service offering to his clients (especially as our local council offers to pay for security locks etc. for all those aged 65 or over) and of course give them peace of mind.

Now do you think he used the idea going forward?

I would say without doubt, no.
Why not, it was a good idea?

I think because he will continue to do what he has always done and introducing my 'Home Security check' would involve him in dialogue with his clients that would take him out of his comfort zone plus he had not been involved in creating it, so little buy in.

However, I still see him advertising for 'new clients' in my local monthly 'glossy ad mag' and indeed the local newspaper, all of which probably costs a few hundred pounds per month. The shame is, growing his average sale would cost him no more than a few sheets of printed A4 paper and have a significant effect on his bottom-line profit.

What would be on your 'service checklist' if you created one?

> **Track your Average Sale on a monthly basis**
> Some accounting software systems can be used to do this automatically (e.g. in Xero look at the Executive report)

> **Come up with six ways to increase your average sale**
> Track the progress you are making on implementing the strategies and the effect on your average sale on a monthly basis

Come Again?

Funnel Management

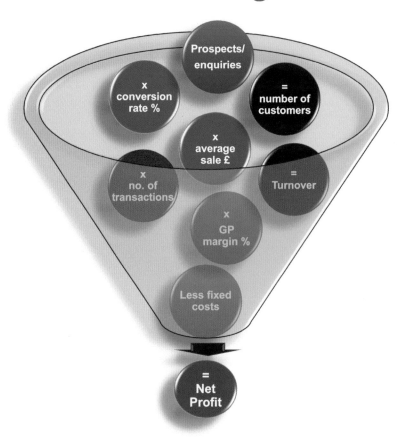

We now move on to our next profitability ball 'Number of Transactions' in essence, getting customers to return and buy again.

What makes you go back to the same restaurant again? Quality of food, service, ambience, convenience, value for money?

Let's consider our good friends McDonalds. Why do people go back there so often (some maybe too often)?

I personally don't think they serve the best burgers in the world, the food served never lives up to the marketing images. I consider, on a peer basis Burger King's offering is better and certainly there are many more places where you can get excellent burgers.

But good old McD's are never short of customers which can be put down to the following:

Consistency – no matter where you are, which restaurant you visit the product offering is consistent (although some products differ by country e.g. the Ebi (prawn) burger in Singapore)
Price – it is always low price
Speed – you know you are going to be tucking into your meal in just a minute or two
Offers – always a 'Meal deal' with a child's toy included (some of the early ones are now collectables)

Amazon are one of the best at getting customers to come back and repurchase. The many 'Recommendations' sent to you based on your previous buying choices, sponsored discounted products, 'Dash Buttons' to make repurchasing easier, deal of the day etc.

These large companies spend a fortune on marketing, but they also know the power of enticing existing customers to buy again – this all fits with the fact that 'habit' and 'trust' are key buying motivators for us all. They also know that happy customers will recommend to others as well as repurchasing themselves.

So, what does this all mean to the smaller business?

Well the start point is that the product or service which the customer originally purchased must have been of sufficient quality and normally reasonably priced* (note not necessarily the cheapest) to make them confident and satisfied with your company.

*A number of high-end products/brands defy the reasonably priced element. A high-end price product, for example a £2000 handbag can psychologically, make the buyer feel much more worthwhile and/or successful because they have purchased something so expensive for what it actually is. They have joined an 'exclusive club'.

Let's assume the customer has purchased from you and was satisfied by the product/service and experience.
The most important thing now is how you follow up on that purchase and this will depend very much on the nature of your business and the frequency at which someone may buy again from you.

For example, an estate agent might sell a home to someone and that customer may move and want to sell the property and buy another after maybe seven years or more. It is still important for that agent to keep in touch, so they are the 'first choice' when that next move occurs and also to gain recommendations from the client. Their retention activities will be very different from the new local restaurant you visited, who should:

- Have offered you to sign up to their email newsletter and offers
- Offered you a complimentary bottle of house wine on your next visit if within a certain period
- Asked you to follow/like them on Facebook/Twitter/Instagram or whatever

In short, ensured that you didn't just walk out of the door leaving them to 'hope' that you come back sometime. Do you think Amazon just 'hope' you come back?

I recall that very first seminar for businesses that I ran in the village where I live. I had invited all local businesses to come along and was delighted that over thirty did so. One of them was a lady who ran a local gift shop selling everything from ornaments, pictures, toys and a small offering of greeting cards.

When I got to the section in the seminar where I covered 'number of transactions' I had asked what activities the attendees used to get people to return. The gift shop lady proudly told me "I have a loyalty card that I give out to encourage people to come back and they get 10% off on subsequent visits.

I congratulated her for this but then pointed out, as someone who has visited the shop on probably half a dozen occasions, that I had never been offered a loyalty card. Her reply pretty much stunned everyone present "No, I only ever give them out to really good customers".

There was then a discussion amongst the attendees as to what was the point in giving them to people who came in regularly and surely you wanted to encourage the less frequent visitor to come in more often?

It's enjoyable and more effective when the audience do the challenging for you!

In reality, every customer should have been offered a loyalty card. If in doubt about offering 10% discount across the board, she could have issued one hundred people with a card and then tested how many revisited against a control group of one hundred without cards.

So, in summary, think about your business/industry, what can you do to get your customers to come back and repurchase?

Does your business have a customer retention strategy?
Consider what would make your customers repurchase from you and produce a plan of activities the business will undertake

Your Rev Counter

Funnel Management

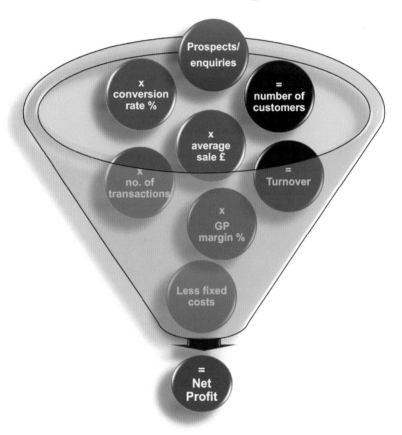

When your child receives their end of term report filled with marks/grades or however the school presents little Johnny or Jennifer's progress you, as parent will expect be invited to come along to discuss the report with their teachers. On the evening you will be given the opportunity to question the teacher(s) on the report marks and comments.

When many business owners get their 'end of term report', their annual accounts, all too often the accounts are emailed out with very little explanation around the numbers/trends and what they might mean.

One of the things that continually amazes me when running Business Growth Seminars is the high percentage of business owners in attendance who, when asked, are not confident in how to calculate gross profit margin and the many who do not know their own 'GP Margin'

The reason it surprises me is that it is such a key number, one of the fundamental 'key performance indicators' of any business. However, I do not consider this to be the fault of those business owners, rather I level the blame for this at the door of their accountants.

Every year businesses pay their accountants sizeable (relatively speaking) fees to produce their annual accounts and I believe the accountants have a duty of care to ensure the owners/directors understand some of these key metrics.

Now I am not having a pop at the accountancy profession as a whole, there are some cracking accountants out there (mine is excellent) but, why do they not all offer the 'Teachers open evening' type opportunity to ensure full understanding?

I do believe that those who do not explain the accounts and key numbers/KPIs to their clients put that business owner at risk. Those explanations should include giving the owner an understanding of what the 'Profit and Loss' and 'Balance sheet' are and how they relate to each other as well as key ratios etc.

Ok so now I have come down from my soapbox, let's look at gross profit margin.

Gross Profit Margin is calculated as follows:

Gross profit i.e. the sales revenue less the cost of sales, divided by the sales revenue x 100

Cost of sales is the variable costs associated with making that sale i.e. any raw material purchased, labour costs (not office staff normally) so by way of example:

A client of mine is a joinery company making wardrobes, kitchens, office storage units etc. Their 'cost of sale' includes purchase cost of materials (wood, fittings etc.) plus the workshop labour costs (Gross wages/National Insurance) of those involved in the actual manufacturing process. It may also include the cost of transporting the products to the customers and installing them.

Another client is in the Public Relations business mostly providing 'services'. They do, however, also undertake events for clients where they will get other companies to build stands or prepare printed literature etc. Their cost of sale would be relatively low but would include all the costs that they incur from 'sub-contracting' out these elements of their sales.

So gross profit is in effect the true income of the business it represents, the income you receive after the cost of you generating that income. So, if you are a sweet shop that buys chocolate bars from a supplier at 30 pence each and sells them for 90 pence then your gross profit is 60 pence per bar.

So why should you also calculate 'gross profit margin?' and why is it useful?

The sale of the chocolate bar above is a gross profit margin of 66.66% which means 66.66% of all the chocolate bars you sell is gross profit (profit before your fixed costs such as rent, utility bills, office salaries etc).

If you track your gross profit margin regularly (normally we would recommend monthly) then any reduction (or indeed increase) should be investigated to understand why. So, let's assume our sweet shop GP margin has dropped, we might find:

- The supplier has put up the cost of chocolate bars
- The bars have been discounted or priced incorrectly
- There has been a rise in theft/shoplifting (shrinkage)
- Some were left out in the sun and have become unsaleable (as I write this, we are experiencing a 30+ degree heatwave in the UK so bear with me!)

A rise in GP margin may mean:
- Your supplier gave you a discount for early settlement of their invoice
- The supplier gave you a discount to take short 'Sell by date' stock
- You have increased prices on the back of my earlier section on average sale!

In short, GP margin is a barometer of how profitably your business is selling its products or services.

If your business was a car then a GP margin dial would most definitely be on the dashboard.

Your Car's Dashboard

Every car has a dashboard – why?

To tell you important information about the car you are driving.

So why not have one for your business?

Numerous clients have found it extremely useful to have one piece of paper which, updated every month, tells you how your business is progressing.

This should include financials, telling you how the business has performed in the last month and year to date, but also give indications of what will happen in the future. For example, it may cover enquiries (potential future customers) or your pipeline (business that may proceed in the short/medium term).

This kind of 'one pager' has enabled a lot of clients to get closer to their numbers without getting completely lost in endless excel spreadsheets or huge 'management packs'

A copy of a typical dashboard is shown overleaf, it includes 'KPIs' (key performance indicators) relevant to that business. Your business will have different KPIs but what's important is that it tracks what is relevant to your business.

If you would like a copy of our 'Dashboard Template' which you can tailor to suit your own business, please feel free to contact us via the details given at the end of the book.

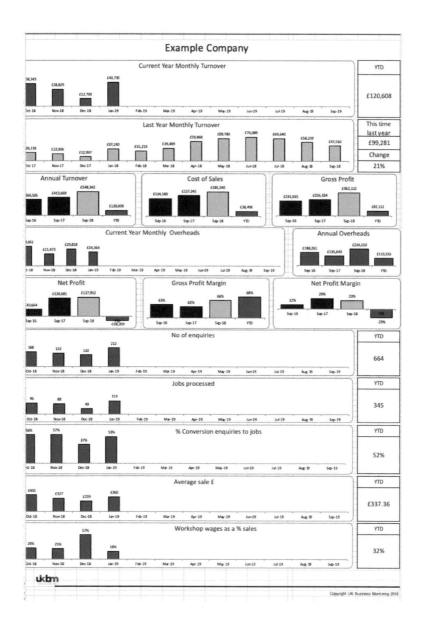

Tracking your business
Have a monthly (weekly if needed) 'Dashboard'
that gives you the information you need to
manage your business. Include the KPIs that are
relevant to your business

Those Monthly Bills

Funnel Management

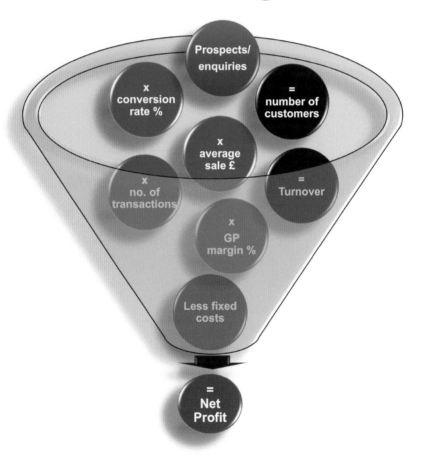

Every business has its regular bills, the ones that come very month/quarter or year, that generally speaking, no matter what sales you make, you have to pay them. These are your 'Fixed costs' also known as indirect costs or overheads - business expenses that are not dependent on the level of goods or services produced by the business.

For the majority of businesses, the two biggest 'fixed costs' will be staff and premises.

I think it was Richard Branson who said that every CEO should every so often look at what bills are being paid every month – it may surprise you – great advice.

When I started my business in 2009, I took premises in Kingston upon Thames Surrey, a small office with a rent of £1,250 per month. It was a serviced office which is nice and easy until you realise that the staff of the serviced office have obviously been to one of our seminars and are always keenly looking at ways to increase their average sale and your monthly spend. "The telephone line is included in the rent; oh, you wanted a phone to go with the line? That will be extra".

After I had established my business, I quickly realised that all of my client meetings were at their premises, not surprisingly I hear you say. The only meetings at my office tended to be people coming to try and sell me something.

I found myself driving, due to traffic, an hour or longer to the office only to sit down and work at a desk. More and more I found myself working from home and eventually came to my senses and invested in a superb 'contemporary garden office' at the bottom of my garden. All paid for in one year from the savings in monthly rent. Commute to work now approximately twenty seconds, longer if I decide to pause to smell the flowers or watch the birds pecking at the fat balls.

Some fixed costs can soon become 'unnecessary' or even a waste and it is always worthwhile running through the fixed costs and asking yourself "Is this really necessary?"

Our involvement with clients has revealed some surprising fixed costs for example:

- £475pm for mobile phones which had been sitting in a drawer for a year
- £1,050pm for a storage yard which stored redundant equipment, all of which had been replaced at some point
- Rent for two floors of a building one of which was not being used, now sublet bringing in £4k per month.
- Numerous subscriptions to online services never used.

In addition, it's always worth reviewing if you are getting the best deal from your suppliers, loyalty is one thing, lethargy is another. All of the following (and more) should be reviewed periodically to ensure you are on the best tariff:

- Utilities (plenty of price comparison sites out there)
- Insurance policies
- Telephones (landlines and mobile)
- Rent – are more cost-efficient premises available elsewhere?
- Bank charges
- Interest on finance/loans
- Leasing/hp/invoice financing
- Vehicle costs
- Etc. Etc.

In short, review all lines!

Sell Enough To Make Nothing

All business owners should know how much their monthly fixed costs are because this then means you can calculate how much you need to sell (or turnover) each month just to cover those costs. This is called your 'breakeven' – the amount you need to sell just to cover fixed costs without making any profit or loss.

The formula for doing this is very simple but known by very few owners:

Monthly fixed costs divided by gross profit margin will give you the level of monthly sales required to 'break even'.

So, if a business has fixed costs of £36,500 per month and its gross profit margin is say 43% then it will need to sell or 'turnover' £84,883 each month to breakeven.

Knowing this figure is invaluable, and every time you increase your fixed costs your breakeven sales figure will increase. So, each time you sign off a new fixed cost or take on a new person in the office, work out your new breakeven, how much more do you now need to sell to cover this new cost?

Getting in the habit of doing this is a great way of making you think 'Do I really need this cost'?

I learned the importance of breakeven in about 1992 on a bank course which included an external speaker 'Brian Warnes' (sadly no longer with us). He showed us this breakeven calculation and would then test us over the five-day course by throwing out a fixed cost figure and GP margin to one of us demanding that we work out the breakeven there and then without a calculator. One of the most challenging courses I have ever attended but boy that formula has stayed with me ever since!

Brian wrote a fabulous book 'The Genghis Khan Guide to Business', well worth a read if you can find a copy.

It can also be useful to know the number of products you need to sell to breakeven - for example if you have worked out that your breakeven sales figure per month is £50,587 and your average product sale is £658 by dividing the former by the latter you will calculate that you have to sell 77 products to breakeven (or 76.879 to the perfectionists amongst you!)

Know your breakeven by number of products
It can also be useful to know the number of products you need to sell to breakeven – for example

If you are in the service industry like me, then just divide the breakeven sales figure by your hourly rate. Therefore, assuming a breakeven sales figure of £10960 and that your hourly rate was say £250, you need to need to 'sell' 44 hours of your service to breakeven.

Feed the Funnel

Funnel Management

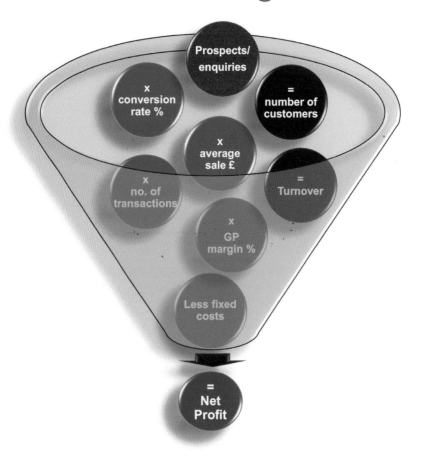

We have now worked through five of the 'profitability balls' and now we shall go back to the first ball 'Prospects'. Just to remind you, this one was left until the end to make the point that it is often easier to improve a business's profitability quickly by focusing on the other areas ahead of marketing for new prospects.

Ball one is Prospects, enquiries, people who walk into your shop, visit your website, call you for a quote or however they might think about doing business with you.
So here is the million-dollar question, how do you get more of them?

Before we start our marketing, we need to understand a few things:

Who is your target market and what are their demographics?

Demographics means 'quantifiable characteristics' what do the people/businesses that normally buy from you have in common?

So, let's go back to our children's nursery example from earlier – their 'clients' may at first sight be the children (Unless two-year olds are now looking after their own finances and I missed it) but obviously the decision makers are the parents. So, what might the demographics of their target market be:

- Parent(s) with children under five
- Male & females where mum is pregnant or thinking of having children (yes people book places before actually becoming pregnant)
- Age group - 16 to 50 (or older these days)
- Living within a reasonable distance of the nursery location (will depend on traffic and area)

- Income – not as relevant due to the Early Years Funding (the Government support scheme) which pays for up to 15 or 30 hours free childcare
- Our nursery is near a main line railway station so could be very useful for parents who commute

Therefore, asking the questions:

Who are they (age/income/interests/jobs etc.)?
Where are they (location/type of property/catchment area)

Enables us to build a picture of the people we are trying to attract.

Another example, albeit in the business to business arena is a client who supplies equipment for commercial kitchens.
Who will his target market be?

Easy enough to list all the restaurants, pubs, hotels within his catchment area but will it be the small independents, or will it be the chains (or both) which ones have purchased from him in the past?

Who in the establishment will be the 'decision maker'? It may well be the owner, the chef, the manager or if a chain maybe the Facilities Manager?

Spending some time reviewing who does business with you now and capturing their common characteristics, enables you to come up with a likely target market for your business. However, don't be limited by who has bought from you in the past, maybe your marketing didn't reach the right audience?

Overlay the above with 'Who benefits from your product or service' or 'Whose problem are you solving?'

My knitwear client who sells £350 cashmere sweaters is not going to target 18-24 year old's (I am sure there are plenty in that age group with money – or parents money but the majority won't spend that on a quality garment with no branded logo or no 'street cred'.

No, his target market is generally 30 – 55-year-old males (its men's knitwear), with reasonable disposable income, living in a nice house in a nice area who recognise a quality garment without the need to have the company name emblazoned across it.

Ok so you have worked out who the target market is and their demographics, the next step is what are the psychographics of that group or 'what are their reasons for buying i.e. their motivation?'

Our knitwear customers would be something like:

"I buy this product because it is a brand, I trust to provide quality garments that look great on, which will last, look good after washing, not pill (no wool or cashmere bobbles all over the sweater) and will keep me warm"

Our younger adults who buy well known recognisable 'trendy' brands might say (if they were honest!) that their reason for buying is:

"I buy this because it makes me feel good about myself, I belong to this 'club' my friends will be impressed that I wear it, it might impress the opposite sex, the logo says something about me"

Interestingly I am told that the population of the UK (mainly the younger ones) are the most obsessed with having a brand or logo on their clothes. In many countries like Spain or Italy (who spend more on clothes per capita than any other country) it is the quality of the garment not the brand.

Why do people buy your service or product? what need, or problem are you solving?

Asking yourself these questions help you to narrow down who it is you want to attract and why they might buy from you.

Now you have worked out your target market and why they might buy from you, it's time to 'market' to them.

What is marketing?

Now if you search marketing on the internet you will find a plethora of information and interpretations, offers, you name it.
I will keep it simple and give you my slant on it:

"Marketing is getting a message about your product or service to people in your target market who may either want or need your product or service"

Let's think about the common ways you might market your business:

Your website – yes but how do you 'market' to get people to your site?

Search engine optimisation (SEO) to attract people searching for your kind of product or service
Google PPC – pay to attract people searching for a particular phrase
Facebook – Use a post or a paid for ad to your target audience (Facebook is very good at allowing you to narrow down your target market with some great demographics)
LinkedIn – posts or ads
You Tube – great for profiling your products or services and also answering the publics questions – "How do I ..."

Instagram – great if you have good visuals
Email to your data base or buy a list of names
Leaflet – drop leaflets through their doors/ in newspapers/ handouts at stations etc.
Telesales (by you, your staff or outsource)
Networking – get out and meet people at organised events
Referrals - get existing clients or contacts to recommend you to other similar people/businesses

There are hundreds of other ways of marketing but these in our experience are the most common.

Some marketing can be undertaken 'inhouse', but some requires technical knowledge, such as SEO or some of the social media advertising mediums.

Our advice is to either undertake some training on the given method if you are going to do it yourself or employ someone to do it for you (who has been recommended) either as an employee or in the early days as an external provider.

The key to any marketing is to track what you do and to measure the success of the campaign against the costs. Track how many new enquiries it brought in and what the conversion rate was and how many sales you achieved on the back of it. Compare it with the costs and work out the 'Client acquisition cost' i.e. how much did you spend in marketing to obtain that client. The next step is to compare the cost of acquisition against the amount of gross profit that client brings you.

Clearly you want the cost of acquisition to be less than the revenue produced!

> **Marketing measurement**
> Test and measure every campaign to
> establish what does and doesn't work

Very few businesses we start working with have any kind of marketing plan, probably less than 20%. There are various reasons for this, lack of time is probably the most common reason, and this is why the next book in the series focusses on managing time and prioritizing as it is a key issue with many business owners.

We hold planning sessions with clients, where we look at their products or services, the demographics of their target market, the psychographics (why they buy) and decide on the best 'marketing routes' to reach that audience.

A typical simple (and the best plans are simple) marketing plan might look like this:

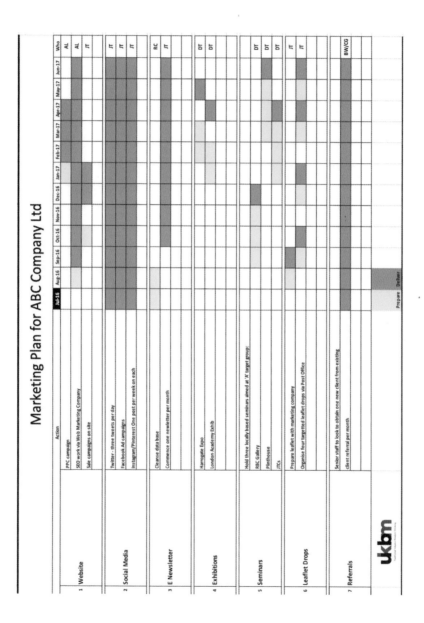

Marketing Plan
Prepare a simple marketing plan outlining
the marketing areas you will focus on,
what you will do and who will do it.
Review it at least monthly.

Adding It All Up

So, if you implemented all the strategies, we have touched on in this book would it make much difference to your business. Hopefully, from some of the examples we have given you will see that it has made a huge difference to some of our clients.

Not surprisingly, whether it makes a difference or not depends largely on how well the owner and his/her staff implement the ideas. For example, I guarantee that if you decide (hopefully you will have already made that decision!) to track your enquiries then you will find that not every enquiry makes its way on to the tracker, other people's idea of what constitutes an enquiry will be different to your own. It does therefore require some managing, some follow up to ensure things happen in the way you want them to, but then again if you're already running a business, I expect you already know that!

When we run seminars on the topics covered in this book, we finish by showing an example of a business's activity figures and what would be the result of improving all of the areas we have covered by just 5%.

Here is that business before any changes are implemented:

Business Dynamics for

Insert % change	Simple Price Change	Prospects	Conversion Rate	Average Sale £	Average Transactions	Gross Profit Margin	Fixed Costs
Prospects	8,000	8,000	8,000	8,000	8,000	8,000	8,000
Conversion Rate	15.0%	15.0%	15.0%	15.0%	15.0%	15.0%	15.0%
Customers	1,200	1,200	1,200	1,200	1,200	1,200	1,200
Average Sale £	£650.00	£650.00	£650.00	£650.00	£650.00	£650.00	£650.00
Average Transactions	1.0	1.0	1.0	1.0	1.0	1.0	1.0
Turnover	£780,000	£780,000	£780,000	£780,000	£780,000	£780,000	£780,000
Gross Profit Margin	55.0%	55.0%	55.0%	55.0%	55.0%	55.0%	55.0%
Gross Profit	£429,000	£429,000	£429,000	£429,000	£429,000	£429,000	£429,000
Fixed Costs	£328,000	£328,000	£328,000	£328,000	£328,000	£328,000	£328,000
Net Profit	£101,000	£101,000	£101,000	£101,000	£101,000	£101,000	£101,000
Action Impact	£0	£0	£0	£0	£0	£0	£0
Cumulative Impact	£0	£0	£0	£0	£0	£0	£0

And the same business after the changes are made:

Business Dynamics for

Insert % change	Simple Price Change	Prospects	Conversion Rate	Average Sale £	Average Transactions	Gross Profit Margin	Fixed Costs
	5%	5%	5%	5%	5%	5%	-5%
Prospects 8,000	8,000	8,400	8,400	8,400	8,400	8,400	8,400
Conversion Rate 15.0%	15.0%	15.0%	15.8%	15.8%	15.8%	15.8%	15.8%
Customers 1,200	1,200	1,260	1,323	1,323	1,323	1,323	1,323
Average Sale £ £650.00	£682.50	£682.50	£682.50	£716.63	£716.63	£716.63	£716.63
Average Transactions 1.0	1.0	1.0	1.0	1.0	1.1	1.1	1.1
Turnover £780,000	£819,000	£859,950	£902,948	£948,095	£995,500	£995,500	£995,500
Gross Profit Margin 55.0%	57.1%	57.1%	57.1%	57.1%	57.1%	60.0%	60.0%
Gross Profit £429,000	£468,000	£491,400	£515,970	£541,769	£568,857	£597,300	£597,300
Fixed Costs £328,000	£328,000	£328,000	£328,000	£328,000	£328,000	£328,000	£311,600
Net Profit £101,000	£140,000	£163,400	£187,970	£213,769	£240,857	£269,300	£285,700
Action Impact	£39,000	£23,400	£24,570	£25,799	£27,088	£28,443	£16,400
Cumulative Impact	£39,000	£62,400	£86,970	£112,769	£139,857	£168,300	£184,700

In summary these 5% improvements have increased net profit by £184,700, an incredible 184% improvement in bottom line profit.

Worthy of an impromptu graphic explosion we feel:

£184,700
Increase in Net
Profit
A 183% Increase!

However, don't just go by what I say, implement some of the ideas and find out for yourself.

You will note that I say 'implement' not 'try' for as Yoda said "Do or do not, there is no try" so execute the changes with rigor and make it happen for your business.

Once you have, please let us know how you got on and the difference(s) it has made for you and your business.

Summary

This little book makes no attempt to teach you everything there is to know about running or growing a small business. What is does attempt to do is give the small business owner some pointers and practical tips on what things you can do to grow and achieve greater profitability. It is perhaps just the starting blocks to getting you moving forward in the journey to grow your creation, your baby, your business.

As previously mentioned, this is the first in a series of small books (manageable chunks – not the whole elephant all at once) aimed at helping the business owner manager to run and grow their business. Ahead of all the books going to print if there is another area you would like help on then please get in touch.

We are here to support any size small business in any industry, if you feel you would like some help and would like to experience a complimentary mentoring session then please feel free to contact us as follows:

Email: joe@ukbusinessmentoring.co.uk

Telephone: **0845 680 3634**

Website: **www.ukbusinessmentoring.co.uk**

My thanks to all the business owners and their staff who have unwittingly contributed to the content of this book over the years.

Thank you for purchasing and reading and I wish you every success in your business.

Printed in Poland
by Amazon Fulfillment
Poland Sp. z o.o., Wrocław

54174892R00063